AlphaZoo
Christmas

This book is dedicated to all the world's animals.
— S.H.

Printed and bound in the United States of America.

Published by Ideals Publishing Corporation
Nashville, Tennessee 37214

Library of Congress Cataloging-in-Publication Data is available.

ISBN 0-8249-8623-7 (trade)
ISBN 0-8249-8632-6 (lib. bdg.)

The illustrations in this book are rendered in watercolors
and colored pencils.
The text type is set in Lower Case Gothic.
The display type is set in Souvenir Light.
Color separations were made by Wisconsin Technicolor Inc.,
New Berlin, Wisconsin.
Printed and bound by Arcata Graphics, Kingsport, Tennessee.

First edition

10 9 8 7 6 5 4 3 2 1

AlphaZoo Christmas

By Susan Harrison

Ideals Children's Books • Nashville, Tennessee

Armadillo
author
addresses
Angora
angels.

a

Boisterous
bluebirds
bake
boysenberry
buns.

b

Caroling
crocodiles
crunch
candy
canes.

D

Dormouse
duo
dreamily
dozes.

d

Elegant
elk
enjoy
excellent
eggnog.

F

Fireside
foxes
festively
fiddle.

Gracious
gecko
gives
guests
gingerbread.

Handsome
hares
harvest
holiday
holly.

I

Interested
iguana
impresses
icy
individual.

J

Juvenile
jaguars
joyfully
jiggle.

j

Kangaroo
kid
kisses
Kringle.

Leder-
hosened
lemur
lightly
leaps.

1

Musing
mandrill
misses
mate's
mistletoe.

Newts
nibble
nutty
nutmeg
nuggets.

Outspoken
owl
organizes
overland
outing.

Plump
pandas
prepare
persimmon
pies.

Quick-
stepping
quetzals
quiet
quintuplets.

Roving
red
reindeer
raise
ruckus.

S

Sweatered
swine
skate
swirling
spirals.

s

Tailored
toads
trade
tiny
teddies.

t

Unsteady
uakari
utilizes
umbrella.

u

Violet-
vested
vicuna
voices
verse.

Waddling
walruses
wear
warm
woollies.

Xeric
xantusia
x-rays
xenops'
xylophone.

Yammering
yaks
yank
yuletide
yew.

Z

Zestful
zebras
zippily
zigzag.

z

GOD IS A SURPRISE

(CHRIST THE KING—Fall)

2 Samuel 5:1-3   Colossians 1:12-20   Luke 23:35-43

THEME
Jesus is a surprise! Both our mighty king and a lowly shepherd.

PROPS
1. A large sign that says "God is a Surprise!"
2. A large cardboard crown attached to a wall or placed on an easel. The children will tape "jewels" onto this crown. The "jewels" are oval, diamond, and hexagon shapes of florist foil and/or colored cellophane.
3. An overhead projector with three to four transparencies (if you have a large group) or pictures (for a smaller group) of "What God looks like to me," drawn by first-grade, third-grade, sixth-grade and ninth-grade students. Also a picture of a king drawn by an older student. These will be used in the lesson.
4. Handouts given to the children are posterboard circles saying "God is a surprise." They should be covered on both sides with clear contact paper. Attach a magnet to the back.

PERSONNEL
1. Presenter
2. Prayer Leader
3. Song Leader
4. Reader
5. 3 students have speaking parts during the dramatic reading of the gospel.

(As the children are greeted at the door, they are given a "jewel" to decorate the crown up front. Adult helpers stand by assisting with glue or tape.)

GREETING

PRESENTER
Today is the feast of Christ the King. I see you've decorated the crown beautifully! A crown is a sign of a king, a rich and powerful person who rules his people. We call Jesus our king. But we also call him the "Good Shepherd," "Our Brother," "Servant of God." A king with such humble titles. How surprising!

OPENING PRAYER

PRAYER LEADER God, oh wondrous Creator, you are beyond the imagination of humankind. Jesus is truly king of our lives, yet he lived as a brother, a shepherd, even as the lamb on the cross. Through Jesus the Christ we give you thanks and praise forever and ever. Amen.

FIRST READING

READER 2 2 Samuel 5:1-3

SONG LEADER "Make a Joyful Noise" (*CTWWS*)

GOSPEL

PRESENTER A dramatic reading of the holy gospel according to St. Luke (23:35-43)

The people stood there watching, and the leaders kept jeering at Jesus, saying:

READER 1 "He saved others; let him save himself if he is the Messiah of God, the chosen one."

PRESENTER The soldiers also made fun of him, coming forward to offer him their sour wine and saying:

READER 2 "If you are the king of the Jews, save yourself."

PRESENTER There was a sign over his head: "This is the King of the Jews." One of the criminals hanging in crucifixion next to him cursed him:

READER 3 "Aren't you the messiah? Then save yourself and us."

PRESENTER But the other one scolded him:

READER 1 "Have you no fear of God, seeing you are suffering the same punishment? We deserve it, after all. We are only paying the price for what we've done, but this man has done nothing wrong."

PRESENTER He then said:

READER 2	"Jesus, remember me when you enter your kingdom.
PRESENTER	And Jesus replied, "I assure you: This day you will be with me in paradise." This is the gospel of the Lord.

LESSON

PRESENTER   In the gospel story it is obvious that Jesus is not what people expected him to be. A "king, hanging on a cross"? That didn't make sense. What did they want to see? How do we "see" God? How do we picture God? Today I have a few pictures drawn by some of our students. They're entitled "What God looks like to me."

First we have a picture from a first-grade student. *(Shows picture or transparency.)* This one is from a third-grader. *(Shows picture or transparency.)* A sixth-grade student drew this one. *(Shows picture or transparency.)* And finally we have a picture from a student in the ninth grade.*(Shows picture or transparency.)*.

They're all different, aren't they? Do you think their idea of God will stay the same as they grow older? No, as we grow, our ideas of God should grow and change too.

In today's first reading we heard about King David being anointed, that is, made king. He was a powerful king. When God's people were waiting for the messiah, the Savior, to come they were expecting a powerful king like David, perhaps like this picture. *(Shows the picture of a king drawn by a student.)* How disappointed and disturbed they were to see their leader die such a death on the cross. Could this be their Savior?

God is a surprise. Our God shows self to us every day in all kinds of ways. Where do you see God? In a church? In a holy picture? When you say your prayers? In your family? In the eucharistic bread? Have you ever looked for God in beautiful sunset, or in trees turning yellow and orange. Have you felt God loving you in a warm smile of a friend or in a gentle touch of a parent? Have you heard God speak to you in Scripture or through your teachers? When we open our minds and hearts, we can see God everywhere!

Let us end our lesson with the song "Surprise" and we will use the motions written for this song. *(See manual accompanying the BWYAP music album.)*

97

SONG LEADER	"Surprise" (*BWYAP*)

COMMUNAL PRAYER

PRAYER LEADER	Our response today is "Lord, hear our prayer."
	Lord, king of our hearts, yet gentle shepherd, teach us to be compassionate and caring to our brothers and sisters, for the needy people in other lands we pray ... Lord, hear our prayer.
	Lord, ever-present God, may we see you everywhere so that we can praise you always and others will see you in us, we pray. Lord, hear our prayer.
SONG LEADER	"Wherever I Am, God Is" (*Hi God III*)